$20.00

03-23-18

REAL HEROES OF SPORTS
HEROIC COMEBACKS

BY JOE TOUGAS

CAPSTONE PRESS
a capstone imprint

Sports Illustrated Kids Stats & Stories are published by Capstone Press,
1710 Roe Crest Drive, North Mankato, Minnesota 56003.
www.mycapstone.com

Library of Congress Cataloging-in-Publication Data
Tougas, Joe, author.
Title: Heroic comeback / by Joe Tougas.
Description: North Mankato, Minnesota : An imprint of Capstone Press, [2017]
 | Series: Sports Illustrated Kids. Real Heroes of Sports. | Includes
 bibliographical references and index. | Audience: Ages: 8-14. | Audience:
 Grades: 4 to 6.
Identifiers: LCCN 2016038719| ISBN 9781515744368 (Library Binding) | ISBN
 9781515744481 (Paperback) | ISBN 9781515744627 (eBook (PDF)
Subjects: LCSH: Athletes—Biography—Juvenile literature. | Athletes—Conduct
 of life—Juvenile literature.
Classification: LCC GV697.A1 T68 2017 | DDC 796.0922 [B]—dc23
LC record available at https://lccn.loc.gov/2016038719

Editorial Credits
Nate LeBoutillier, editor; Terri Poburka, designer;
Eric Gohl, media specialist; Gene Bentdahl, production specialist

Photo Credits
AP Photo: 7, 27 (top), Marcio Jose Sanchez, 12; Capstone: cover (bottom left & bottom
right), 1; Getty Images: Popperfoto, 16; Newscom: Everett Collection, 14, 15, ZUMA
Press/Allen Eyestone, 9 (bottom); Shutterstock: Daniel Schweinert, cover (top right),
Lev Radin, 27 (bottom), Miceking, cover (top left); Sports Illustrated: Al Tielemans,
13 (top), Bill Frakes, 23 (top), Bob Martin, 26, Bob Rosato, 22, 23 (bottom), Damian
Strohmeyer, 21 (top right & bottom), David E. Klutho, 20, 24, 25, John G. Zimmerman,
6, 28, 29, Lane Stewart, 5, Robert Beck, 13 (bottom), 21 (top left), Simon Bruty, 10, 11,
Tony Triolo, 8, 9 (top), Walter Iooss Jr., 17, 18, 19
Design Elements: Shutterstock

Printed in the United States of America.
010054S17

Table of
CONTENTS

WHEN WINNING IS AGAINST THE ODDS

Every now and then, great athletes will show the world something more than remarkable skills in a game. They will show how important it is to still believe in yourself, even if you have been set back by illness, injury, or defeat.

These are the athletes who don't listen to those who doubt. They hit the court, the field, the track, or the slopes ready to do their absolute best. When they shock the world with amazing triumphs, they are praised for making a great "comeback." By overcoming problems and believing in themselves above all, they become more than champions of their sport. They become great examples—heroes, even—to fans who have faced long odds and tough challenges in their lives.

Muhammad ALI:

Stung Like a Bee

A young fighter named Cassius Clay began boxing in Kentucky and won the Olympic gold medal in Rome in 1960 as an 18-year-old. He went on to become heavyweight champion of the world by age 22 and changed his name to Muhammad Ali while converting to the Islamic faith.

Soon the Vietnam War was raging, and, like many young Americans, Ali received a draft notice. Ali, however, refused to be drafted into the United States military. He cited religious reasons of his newfound Islamic faith.

Though he could not be made to go to war, Ali paid a high price.

Muhammad Ali as an Olympian

Muhammad Ali speaks to the Illinois Athletic Commission in 1966.

Heroic FACT

Due to suspension, Muhammad Ali did not box between the ages of 25 years and 65 days and 28 years and 281 days. The mid-to-late 20s are generally considered an athlete's prime.

A federal grand jury sentenced him to five years in prison for draft evasion. In 1967 the boxing commission took away Ali's title as champion and suspended him from fighting. At the time, Ali was undefeated at 29-0 at the age of 25.

Ali appealed. As he fought his case in the courts, he continued to speak out against the Vietnam War. Eventually, the Supreme Court reversed Ali's conviction.

In 1970 Ali's boxing suspension was lifted. He never went to prison, but he hadn't been in the ring in three years. Ali's first fight to regain the heavyweight title came in March of 1971, at age 29. In a fight deemed "The Fight of the Century," Ali was defeated—for the very first time—in 15 rounds by Joe Frazier. Frazier himself was unbeaten entering the fight.

Ali refused to give up on his comeback.

He fought his way up through ranks to defeat Frazier and George Foreman in a pair of thrilling 1974 fights, and he recaptured his undisputed heavyweight title. More victories followed as Ali became a household name and one of America's greatest sports heroes.

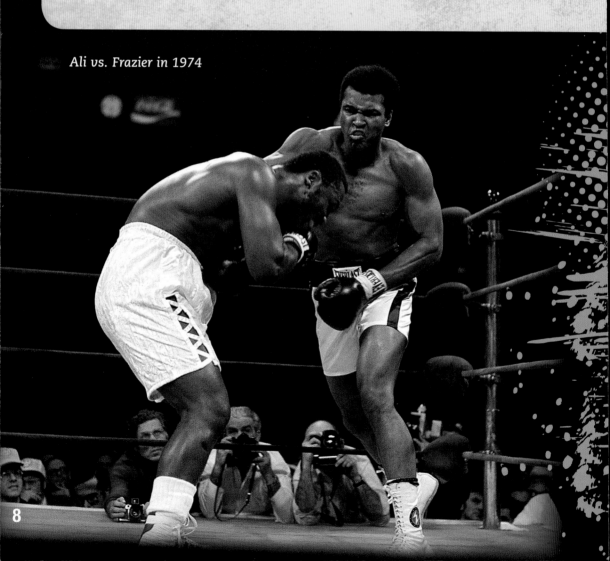

Ali vs. Frazier in 1974

At the end of his career, Ali had time for one more comeback. After losing his title to Leon Spinks in 1978, he came back later in the year to face Spinks in a rematch. This time, the 36-year-old Ali beat Spinks in a unanimous decision to regain the undisputed heavyweight title. The victory, Ali's last, ran his impressive record to 56-3.

Ali remains the only boxer who held the title of heavyweight champion three separate times. He died in 2016 at age 74.

BRAVE FIGHT:
ALI VS. PARKINSON'S

As the world looked on, a visibly shaking Muhammad Ali lit the Olympic torch in Atlanta to touch off the 1996 Olympic Games. By this time, Ali had been living with Parkinson's disease for 12 years. He was lauded by Parkinson's research advocates for going public with his condition and later founded the Muhammad Ali Parkinson Center in Phoenix.

Lindsey
VONN:

Downhill Racing, Uphill Climbs

Two weeks before she was to ski in the 2010 Vancouver Olympics, World Cup winner Lindsey Vonn hurt her leg seriously during training. The pain in her swollen shin caused many, including Vonn, to worry whether she would be able to compete.

Vonn not only competed but became the first American to win the gold in women's downhill skiing. It was an amazing comeback, and she followed it up with another World Cup title in 2012.

Vonn would face one more major challenge—and triumph. During the 2013 World Championships in Austria, Vonn suffered a wipeout in the Super G that caused torn ligaments and a fracture in her right knee. Surgery helped, but she damaged the same leg later that year, forcing her to miss the 2014 Olympics.

She returned to the slopes in January of 2015. Wasting no time, she won her 63rd World Cup event, setting the record for most World Cup wins. She also holds the record with 20 World Cup overall titles, as well, and is preparing for the 2018 Olympics.

Heroic FACT

Though Lindsey Vonn was forced to miss the 2014 Olympics in Sochi, Russia, she covered Olympic competition as a correspondent for NBC.

Lindsey Vonn at the 2010 Winter Olympics

Buster
POSEY:
Crash Course

It was the 12th inning, and San Francisco Giants catcher Buster Posey had two objects hurtling toward him. One was a ball sailing in high from right field. The other, to his left, was the sprinting body of Scott Cousins of the Florida Marlins. Cousins charged at the catcher with the intent of scoring by knocking Posey down.

Their fierce collision sent Posey flying, breaking the fibula in his left leg and dislocating his ankle. The injury took place in 2011, a year after Posey had been named 2010 Rookie of the Year and caught for the Giants in the World Series. In his surgery, two screws were inserted into his left leg to help support his ankle. He recovered in time to return the following season and help the Giants win the 2012 World Series. He also took home the National League Most Valuable Player award.

KNOCK IT OFF

Buster Posey's injury prompted Major League Baseball to make some changes. In 2014 they made a rule to try and prevent violent home plate collisions. Today, runners cannot stray from their path in order to knock over a catcher, and catchers cannot stand in the way of a runner unless they have the baseball.

Heroic FACT

Posey was named the National League Comeback Player of the Year in 2012, as well as the league's Most Valuable Player. He batted .336 that year, tops in the Majors.

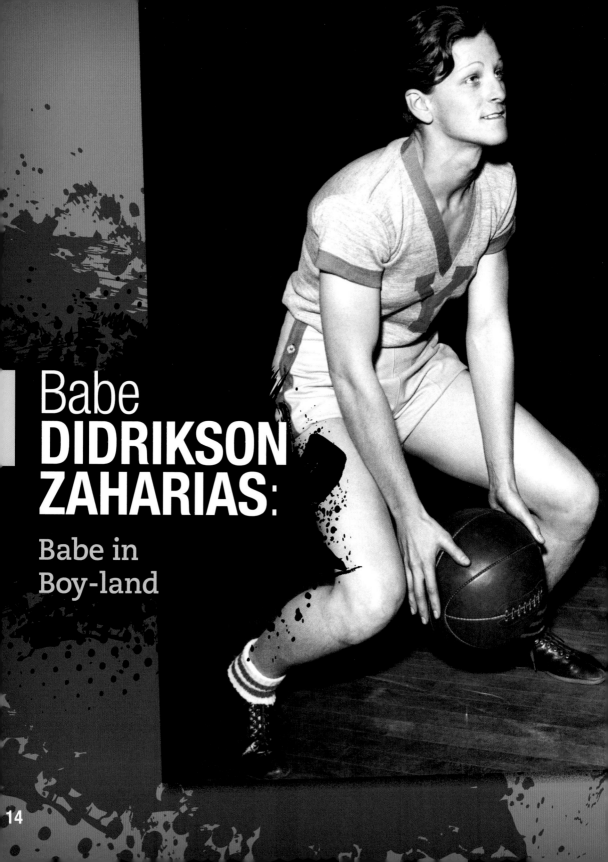

Babe
DIDRIKSON
ZAHARIAS:

Babe in
Boy-land

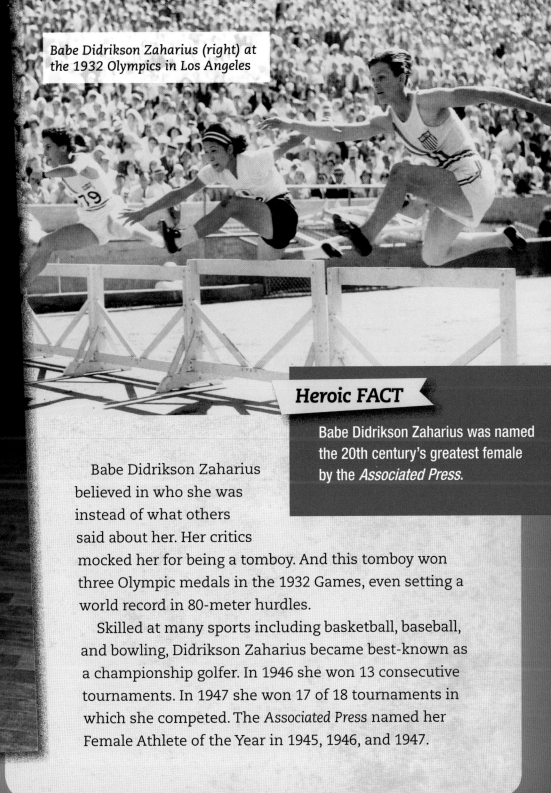

Babe Didrikson Zaharius (right) at the 1932 Olympics in Los Angeles

Babe Didrikson Zaharius believed in who she was instead of what others said about her. Her critics mocked her for being a tomboy. And this tomboy won three Olympic medals in the 1932 Games, even setting a world record in 80-meter hurdles.

Skilled at many sports including basketball, baseball, and bowling, Didrikson Zaharius became best-known as a championship golfer. In 1946 she won 13 consecutive tournaments. In 1947 she won 17 of 18 tournaments in which she competed. The *Associated Press* named her Female Athlete of the Year in 1945, 1946, and 1947.

While many described her as a great example of muscle and mental coordination, Didrikson Zaharius herself was matter-of-fact about her golfing skills. "You've got to loosen your girdle and let it rip," she once explained. And let it rip she did. In 1948 Didrikson Zaharius won the women's U.S. Open, the World Championship, and the All-American Open. She was so dominant that she attempted to qualify for the men's U.S. Open, but her application was rejected due to her gender.

Didrikson at the 1947 British Women's Amateur Golf Championship

In 1953 Didrikson Zaharius developed cancer in her lymph nodes, which was deemed incurable at the time. Although she called it the toughest competition she had ever faced, she did not let cancer stop her drive. Fourteen weeks after being diagnosed, Didrikson Zaharius came back to win her third women's U.S. Open, along with five other titles that year. And once again, she was selected as the *Associated Press*'s Female Athlete of the Year. In September of 1956, she died in a hospital in Galveston, Texas.

LIGHTNING-STRENGTH COMEBACK

In 1974 golfer Lee Trevino won his first PGA Championship. The next year, he was struck by lightning at a tournament. Despite back problems and surgeries afterward, Lee came back to win the PGA Championship 10 years later in 1984. Considered by many to be the greatest Hispanic-American golfer in history, Trevino won 29 PGA Tour events, including six majors.

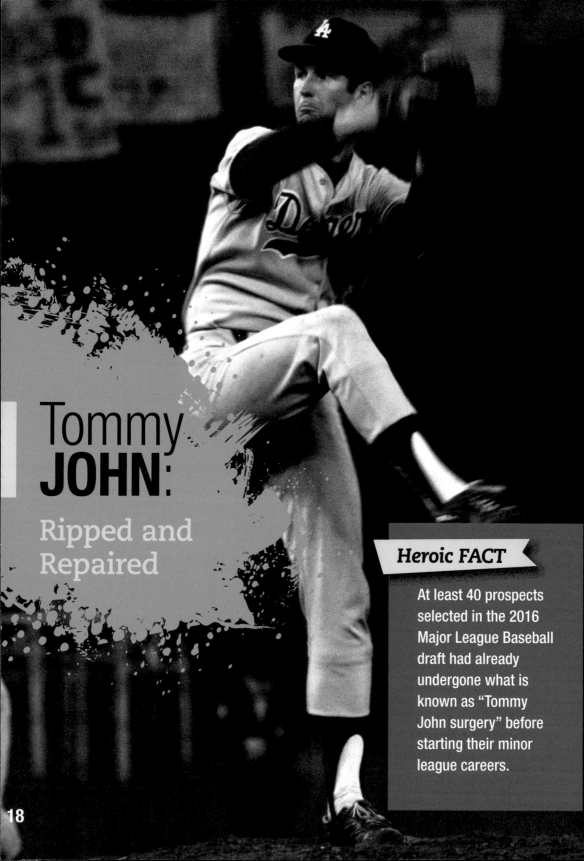

Tommy JOHN:

Ripped and Repaired

Heroic FACT

At least 40 prospects selected in the 2016 Major League Baseball draft had already undergone what is known as "Tommy John surgery" before starting their minor league careers.

Tommy John and manager Tommy Lasorda in the 1977 playoffs

It was the fourth inning of a 1974 professional baseball game between the Los Angeles Dodgers and the Montreal Expos. Dodgers pitcher Tommy John was on the mound and delivered a pitch. Something popped, and John had to come out of the game. He would later say it felt as though his pitching arm left his body. It wasn't painful—his arm simply had no feeling at all.

The 31-year-old John had damaged the ligament that connected his forearm to his upper arm. In the past, this same injury had forced many pitchers to quit the game. John was lucky to have a surgeon with a new idea. To repair John's pitching arm, Doctor Frank Jobe used a tendon from John's right wrist to replace the torn tendon on his left elbow. This surgery was the first of its kind.

John not only continued playing, but he improved his pitching prowess post-surgery. He won another 164 games in 14 seasons before retiring at age 46 in 1989.

Peyton **MANNING** and Tom **BRADY**:

From the Ground Up

In 2011 Peyton Manning went from being the best quarterback in the game to needing to re-learn everything about throwing a football. Two surgeries to fix his back and neck had weakened his right arm and fingers dramatically. Manning was determined to get his arm back, even when his first throws following surgery went only five yards. His aim was off, and the longtime quarterback in his mid-30s privately wondered if he would ever play the game again. Manning trained constantly and patiently, gradually recovered his passing skills. Joining the Denver Broncos, Manning led them to a 13-3 season in 2012. The following year, while taking the Broncos to their Super Bowl win, Manning broke records for passing touchdowns and passing yards. He also earned that year's NFL MVP award. His is considered the most impressive injury comebacks of all time.

Peyton Manning on the sidelines in 2011

Peyton Manning

Tom Brady

KNOCKED DOWN AND SOARING UP

Fresh from winning the 2007 MVP award, New England Patriots quarterback Tom Brady saw his 2008 season cut extremely short. In the Patriots' first game of the season, Brady took a hit and tore three knee ligaments. He missed the rest of the season but returned to win the 2009 NFL Comeback Player of the Year award and NFL Most Valuable Player in 2010.

Tom Brady after injury in 2008

Alonzo
MOURNING:
New Mourning in Hoops

Miami Heat center Alonzo Mourning had many people to thank during his 2014 Hall of Fame induction speech. He thanked coaches who helped him learn, teammates who helped him grow, and the cousin who helped him live.

In 2000 the NBA All-Star and gold medal Olympian began feeling run-down. He learned that he had a kidney condition but tried playing through it. By 2003 Mourning decided to retire when doctors told him he was risking heart failure by continuing to play. As the condition worsened, Mourning learned he would need a kidney transplant to survive.

After searching for a donor, it was determined that Jason Cooper, Mourning's cousin, was a match. Cooper donated one of his kidneys to save the hoops star's life. Mourning's recovery was slow after the December 2003 surgery, but he was determined. Mourning returned to the court in 2004. In 2006 he helped the Heat win the NBA championship.

At his 2014 Hall of Fame induction speech, Mourning thanked his cousin for "the most generous thing one person could do for another. Give a piece of themselves."

Alonzo Mourning raising the NBA Championship trophy

Heroic FACT

Jason Cooper was a former U.S. Marine. Before Mourning's kidney transplant, the two had not seen each other for 25 years.

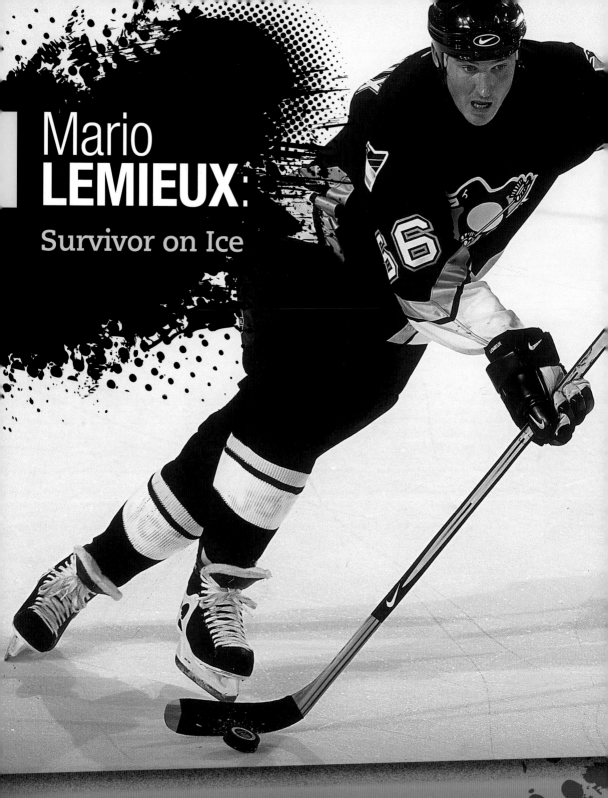

Mario
LEMIEUX:
Survivor on Ice

Cancer struck Mario Lemieux one year after he led the Pittsburgh Penguins to their 1992 Stanley Cup win. To fight the disease, the 28-year-old Lemieux had to take two months off in 1993 for radiation treatment. He returned to the game on the last day of his treatment and went on to be the season's top scorer—even after missing 20 games.

He retired in 1997 and became part-owner of the Penguins in his early 30s. But after three years, he announced he would return to the game. This second comeback lasted five seasons, during which he scored 229 points. During that period of time, Lemieux also captained Team Canada to a gold medal at the 2002 Olympics, scoring a stunning six goals in five games.

His return to hockey stunned the sports world. It also prompted *Hockey News* writer Tom Thompson to write, "Lemieux's comeback was the most remarkable feat of its kind in my lifetime."

Mario Lemieux (center) as an Olympian in 2002

Heroic FACT

Mario Lemieux was bestowed the title of knight from Quebec Premier Jean Charest in 2009.

Monica
SELES:
A Comeback Kid

At 16 Monica Seles won the French Open tennis tournament, and she went on to win seven of the next 11 Grand Slam competitions. But her promise was halted in 1993 when a spectator stabbed Seles in the back as she sat courtside during a break in play. Seles was the victim of a crazed fan of rival player Steffi Graf. The man was arrested at the scene, but Seles suffered a serious injury.

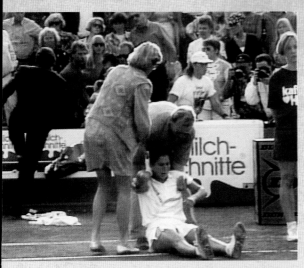
Monica Seles after being stabbed in 1993

Seles couldn't play in any more tournaments that year. She spent the next two years working to heal not only her injury but also the anxiety and depression that came from both the stabbing as well as her father's failing health. Therapy and outside activities such as skydiving and traveling would help her to eventually overcome her fears and troubles.

She returned to the game in 1995. That year Seles dominated the Canadian Open and won another Grand Slam competition at the Australian Open. She then battled her way to the U.S. Open championship against her old rival, Graf. Seles lost the match by a score of 7-6, 0-6, 6-3. But her return and rise inspired fans and players around the world.

DOWN BUT NEVER OUT

As the winner of the most major victories in the history of women's pro tennis, Serena Williams is no stranger to comebacks. Thirty-three times in Grand Slam matches (Wimbledon, French Open, U.S. Open, and Australian Open), she has come back from one set down to claim victory.

Serena Williams

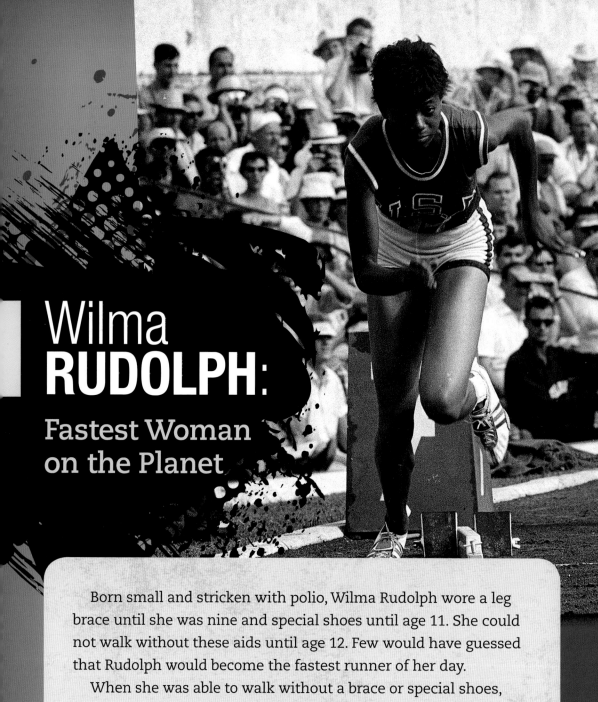

Wilma
RUDOLPH:
Fastest Woman on the Planet

Born small and stricken with polio, Wilma Rudolph wore a leg brace until she was nine and special shoes until age 11. She could not walk without these aids until age 12. Few would have guessed that Rudolph would become the fastest runner of her day.

When she was able to walk without a brace or special shoes, Rudolph enjoyed playing several different sports. Despite her history of leg problems, she ran so fast in track that, in 10th grade, she was invited to join the summer track program of Tennessee State University.

Wilma Rudolph at the 1960 Olympics

Following her success in that program, Rudolph made it onto the United States Olympic team. In 1956 she won a bronze medal in the 4 x 100 meter sprint relay.

She continued to work hard at running for the next four years. In the 1960 Rome Olympics, she won gold medals in three different race events, the first American woman to ever do so. At age 20, this once sickly and polio-stricken child suddenly had the world's attention as the fastest woman alive.

Heroic FACT

Wilma Rudolph was born in St. Bethlehem, Tennessee, on June 23, 1940, and weighed only 4.5 pounds. She was the 20th of her father's 22 children.

Glossary

anxiety — a feeling of worry or fear

draft — to select young men to serve in the military

ligament — a band of tissue that connects bones to bones

prejudice — an opinion about others that is unfair or not based on facts

radiation —rays of energy given off by certain elements

rival — someone whom a person competes against

segregation — separating people because of their skin color

tomboy — a girl who enjoys rough, noisy activities usually associated with boys

triumph — a great victory or achievement

Vietnam War — the conflict from 1954 to 1975 between South Vietnam and North Vietnam in which at least 50,000 American soldiers died

Read More

Knudson, R. R. Knudson. *Babe Didrikson: Athlete of the Century* Women of Our Time. New York: Puffin Books, 2015.

Peters, Gregory. *Muhammad Ali Boxing Legend.* North Mankato, Minn.: Capstone Press, 2013.

Weakland, Mark. *When Wilma Rudolph Played Basketball.* North Mankato, Minn.: Capstone Press, 2016.

Internet Links

FactHound offers a safe, fun way to find Internet sites related to this book. All of the sites on FactHound have been researched by our staff.

Here's all you do:

Visit *www.facthound.com*

Type in this code: 9781515744368

Check out projects, games and lots more at
www.capstonekids.com

Index